Partner Swapping - Are You Ready?

An Interactive Guide/Workbook for Couples

L.A. Theriault

DEDICATION

This book is dedicated to the friends I love and my partner, the love of my life.

CONTENTS

ACKNOWLEDGMENTS

Thank you to all of my friends and family. For some reason, they believe in me, and for that I am always grateful.

1 TAKING THE LEAP

Use this book to open the dialogue between you and your partner. Keep an open mind and pay particular attention to anything in this book that causes you to cringe. If there's anything in this book that you don't feel comfortable discussing, answering honestly or even thinking about, it could be your red flag to reconsider. Partner swapping is a big deal. It can add excitement to your relationship, but it can also tear your relationship apart.

Couples don't usually just wake up one morning and decide to "do" the neighbors. In fact, the decision can arise out of any number of situations that are unique to that couple. In each of the following chapters there are a series of questions designed to really get to the heart of the matter. Pay attention to your responses and how you feel as you answer the questions with your partner. Does the conversation feel tense or do you feel safe in expressing your concerns, desires, wishes, and wants? Be aware of any moments of tension or discomfort. This means that there needs to be more conversation around that topic before taking the partner swapping plunge.

This book isn't designed to judge or convince couples not to engage in partner swapping. It's simply a vehicle to help people decide if the lifestyle is right for them.

Is it right for you? There are two ways to find out: 1) Jump into partner swapping without any thought and deal with any issues later; 2) Read the book, answer the questions honestly and thoughtfully, and make an informed decision.

2 REASONS

The idea of partner swapping is exciting. Sometimes just thinking about it is enough to recharge the intimacy in your relationship. The reality is that thinking about partner swapping means that there's something going on either in yourself or in your relationship. Looking for new partners to have sex with doesn't mean there's anything wrong with you but it could be a sign that your relationship needs some fine-tuning.

Pick a time when you and your partner are relaxed and have the time to share the following questions. Don't feel as if you have to cover all of the questions in this book. Instead, look at the questions that really jump out at you and see what kind of conversation comes from it. These questions are designed to help guide an intimate conversation about what you want from your relationship.

1) Why do we want to engage in partner swapping?

2) Do I feel pressured, bullied, or coerced into partner swapping?

3) Am I thinking about partner swapping as a way out of this relationship?

4) What do I hope to gain from this experience?

5) Do I believe that the act of sex can be distinctly separate from love and intimacy?

6) Am I considering partner swapping because there's one person in particular that I want to be intimate with?

7) Is partner swapping a way to "cheat" without feeling like I'm really cheating?

8) Do we want to engage in partner swapping as a way of reliving the "honeymoon phase" of our own relationship?

9) Do we want to engage in partner swapping because other people we know are doing it?

10) Are we still in love with each other?

How did that go? These aren't easy questions to answer but in the interest of protecting your relationship and your sanity, it's important to go through this process. Partner swapping means different things to different people. For some, it means choosing another couple that you know well and trust implicitly. It might be a one-time thing or it could evolve into an alternative relationship where you have your spouse/partner and a boyfriend/girlfriend on the side. Remember, we're not talking about cheating; this is about full disclosure and acceptance of a full swapping partnership.

Sometimes you need to take a long, hard look at your relationship. It's easy to say that you're just looking for some mutually agreed upon sexual fun with another couple when what you really mean is, "I don't want to be with you anymore and I'm looking for a way out." If your conversation comes to that realization, close the book and take a deep breath. Some painful emotions can arise from realizations like this. At this point, talk about what you want to do next. Couples counseling? A trial separation? Or maybe you'll just decide to engage in partner swapping in the hopes that it will bring you closer together. The decisions are all yours, just take your time and make sure both parties are in total agreement going forward.

By being honest with yourself and your intentions, you can save yourself a lot of unnecessary grief down the road.

As you go through the next set of questions, allow your partner ample time to express and articulate his or her thoughts. Give each other some space, jot down notes, walk away and come back – whatever you both have to do to make the most of this experience. Respect and understand that the answers you get might not be the answers you expected.

3 BOUNDARIES

Before embarking on a partner swapping relationship, set boundaries. Partner swapping seems pretty simple. You pick a couple, sleep with them, and then it's over, right? Not really. Your definition of partner swapping might be completely different from your partner's definition. There's actually a lot to think about and these are the kinds of questions that should be discussed at length:

1) What does partner swapping mean to me?

2) Does partner swapping mean full penetration?

3) Is deep kissing okay?

4) Is anal sex okay?

5) Will we always use condoms or dams to protect ourselves from sexually transmitted diseases?

6) Will we swap partners in the same room together or in different rooms?

7) Is partner swapping something we will always engage in together with another mutually agreed upon couple, or is this opening the gates to "free" swapping whenever we want?

8) If one of us wants to stop partner swapping permanently – no questions asked – are we ready to accept and respect that decision?

9) What do I constitute as "abuse" and what am I not willing to tolerate?

10) Do we agree not to discuss personal matters about our own relationship with the swapping partners?

These aren't easy questions to answer, but they'll go a long way in determining how far you're willing to go. Use the contract on the next page to help make sure both you and your partner fully understand what you will and will not accept when engaging in partner swapping activities. You can also use the template as a guideline to create your own contract.

OUR PERSONAL BOUNDARIES CONTRACT

Entered into by (names of partners)

_____

_____

On this date:_____

I _____ *agree that it is acceptable for us both to engage in the following activities keeping in mind that if either of us want to end partner-swapping, we only have to say "I want this to end". At that point, we will both not engage in further partner swapping activities:*

1.

2.

3.

4.

I _____ *also agree that it is acceptable for us both to engage in the following activities keeping in mind that if either of us want to end partner-swapping, we only have to say "I want this to end". At that point, we will both not engage in further partner swapping activities.*

1.

2.

3.

4.

4 JEALOUSY

Fantasizing about your partner having sex with someone else is one thing, but when it actually happens, reality can hit hard. Once you've engaged in partner swapping you can't turn back. You can end the activities if you choose but you can't erase what's already been done. Are you sure you're going to be okay with it? Insecurities you never thought existed can tear away at your sanity and your relationship. It's easy to say its "just sex" and that it doesn't mean anything, but what it really amounts to is sharing your partner's intimate, most primal self with another person.

Have a look at the following set of questions and take some time to discuss your thoughts, fears, and insecurities with your partner:

1) How do I define jealousy?

2) Am I a "jealous" person?

3) What feelings (anger, sadness, fear, etc.) arise when I experience feelings of jealousy and how do I deal with them?

4) What am I most afraid of when I think of partner swapping?

5) Should feelings of jealousy be a reason to discontinue partner swapping?

6) Are feelings of jealousy going to be too much for me to handle?

7) What are some meaningful ways of reassuring each other to ease feelings of insecurity?

8) Am I emotionally ready to partner-swap?

9) Am I happy with who I am as a person?

10) Do I accept my own perceived physical flaws?

Jealousy is an insidious reaction to our own fears and insecurities. Partner swapping should be a fun, safe, exciting, and interesting way of bringing pleasure into your own relationship. Unfortunately, feelings of jealousy can thwart that. Take some time to discuss how you might feel and react to the reality of swapping partners and what you might do to alleviate those feelings. The gurus of the world might say that jealousy is a useless emotion. The reality is that whether it's useless or not, jealousy sometimes coils its way through our core, tainting the way we view ourselves and our relationships. The best way to avoid this is to avoid situations that might nurture this stress-inducing emotion. Sometimes one partner might insist he or she isn't the "jealous type" without really thinking about what that means. The desire to engage in new, exciting, "forbidden" sexual activity can easily override common sense, which is why it's important to sit back and really think about the implications.

Jealousy can quickly escalate from quiet anxiety to murderous rage. It can simmer within; creating a host of stress-related symptoms in the body or it can manifest itself in counterproductive, harmful behavior. Jealousy has been demonstrated in professional level sports where athletes have purposely sabotaged the efforts of their rivals. Corporations have used nefarious means to undermine competitors. While there any number of excuses for these behaviors, it's likely the aggression stems from the seed of jealousy.

Partner-swapping seems like a great idea in theory until you start to over-analyze that situation. Doubts and insecurities creep into the subconscious. Do I look better than he or she does? Is he or she a better lover than I am? I wonder if he or she shares the same interests as my partner. What if my partner decides to leave me for him or her? These are all reasonable questions because no matter how committed and strong your relationship is, the integrity of it is compromised with every new sexual partner allowed past the gate. The question is, can you handle it? Can you handle the doubts and insecurities that could follow?

5 DISCRETION

Admit it, after a few drinks you'll say just about anything to anyone. Maybe you really don't care if word gets around the officee that you're into partner swapping and maybe you couldn't care less whether crazy Aunt Matilda whispers her "news" into the ears of the same people who teach your children in elementary school. The reality is, there's always the chance that word is going to get out and there's not much you can do about it.

All of the soul-searching in the world isn't going to stop you, your partner, or anyone else from discussing the intimate details of your sexual encounters. The reality is that it shouldn't matter how consenting adults conduct their personal lives. If it's legal and isn't hurting anybody else, it shouldn't be anyone's business. Of course we know that isn't the way the world works. People have lost jobs over compromising photographs discovered on social networking sites. Like it or not, we're living in a highly publicized digital age where the average Joe can find himself publicly scandalized because of a seemingly innocuous comment or photograph uploaded to Facebook®.

Take some time to discuss the questions below with your partner. There's no way of guaranteeing discretion in anything you do these days, but this might help you to gain an understanding of the possibilities and what you might do to maintain your own privacy.

1) Do you use any of the social networking sites?

2) Do you understand how to set up the security parameters on your networking sites?

3) Do you realize that friends of friends can still find their way to your information through the "back door"?

4) How well do you know the people you're planning to partner swap with and can you trust them to keep your intimate interactions discreet?

5) Do you have children and, if so, how might the knowledge of your personal lives impact theirs?

6) What steps will you and your partner take to protect your privacy?

7) Are there people in your life that you would not want to find out about your partner swapping activities? Who are they and why is it important that they not find out.

8) How will you keep your partner swapping activities from certain people?

9) Are you comfortable with lying if necessary?

10) Can you trust your own partner to be discreet?

It's a fine-line between not caring what people think of us, and the reality of our private lives suddenly becoming public in a way that can destroy families and careers. As much as social networking sites have opened our worlds in a good way, allowing us to communicate openly and freely with people we might not have otherwise connected with, there's also a dangerous side that we've allowed to happen. Unsuspecting people have sat themselves in the middle of a proverbial Petri dish, exposed every private thought and action, and then opened the pubic lens as wide as possible. Through our own doing, nothing is private anymore.

6 PREGNANCY & STD'S

Okay, let's get really scary here. What if you get pregnant? There are many birth control options, but none of them are foolproof. Condoms break, birth control pills are forgotten, and (although rare) even vasectomies have been known to reverse. Is having someone else's baby something you're willing to take on, or are you going to have abortion should that happen. It's not a pleasant topic to think about within the context of partner swapping; it's pretty scary stuff actually. The reality is that it could happen and if it does, are you prepared to deal with it?

Equally frightening is the possibility of contracting sexually transmitted diseases (STD's). Of course you already know that wearing a condom is vital to protecting yourself against STD's, but they're not foolproof. Besides abstinence, condoms are the best way to help protect yourself from nasty and sometimes life-threatening STD's.

Read through the following questions with your partner to explore the possibilities and realities of an unplanned pregnancy.

1) What will happen if I get pregnant?

2) Will you support me if I have someone else's baby?

3) Am I okay with having an abortion?

4) If I keep the baby, what would we tell our family?

5) Do I have any health conditions that would make it dangerous to carry a baby to full term?

6) Are we planning on using condoms, in addition to any other birth control methods, as a way of reducing the possibility of pregnancy and protecting ourselves against sexually transmitted diseases (STD's)?

9) Do I have any STD's that I'm aware?

10) Should I disclose any STD's to sexual partners?

The reality is that if you knowingly have something as serious and life-threatening as HIV and have unprotected sex with a partner without telling them your health situation, you could be charged with a serious crime should that person contract HIV.

If you and your partner are going to engage in the swapping lifestyle, please discuss and disclose any and all health problems with your partners. Okay, they might not care about the ear infection you just had, but you get the picture. Keep it real. Don't try to hide anything from anybody. Use condoms   every   time.

7 EMOTIONAL ATTACHMENTS

Couples who decide to get into partner-swapping sometimes do it to bring the spark back into their own sex lives. You may even feel yourself loving your partner even more in the early days of partner swapping, for giving you this "freedom" and trust. Sharing yourself in a sexually intimate way with another person invites complex emotions to surface. Suddenly you're discussing things with the other person (thoughts, dreams, goals, aspirations) that you don't even share with your own spouse. Suddenly the other person seems more understanding and accepting of you. Of course he/she does! They only have to see you once in a while without having to share the responsibilities of the household. It's easy to see someone as having a glowing halo when they're not complaining that you never clean the grout out of the shower. But you don't think of that. All you can think of is that smiling, attentive person that you've been having sex with and nothing else. Emotions rise to the surface. Are you falling in love? This is where partner-swapping really gets into dangerous territory. This is where it might be a good idea to schedule some time to communication with your wife/husband/partner.

Answer the following questions as a way of opening the dialogue with your partner. Talk about ways in which you might keep the recreational sex where it belongs, and the emotional attachments where they belong – in your own relationship.

1) Are we planning on swapping with friends we already know or strangers?

2) Will our swapping activities be with the same couple all of the time, or will we swap with different partners most of the time?

3) How much do I trust that my partner loves and respects me?

4) By partner swapping, I'm agreeing to let my wife/husband/boyfriend/girlfriend have sex with another person. What don't I want him/her to share with the other person? What things about my life do I want to keep private?

5) Should we promise not to use the other sexual partner as a sounding board for whatever problems might be going on in our own relationship?

6) Outside of sex, what do we define as "getting too close" to the swapping partners?

7) How do we draw and define the line so that recreational sexual activity doesn't threaten our own relationship? For example, should we notify each other if one of the swapping partners tries to contact us privately?

8) Can we regularly have time that's just for us as a way of reconnecting to what makes our own relationship special and unique?

9) Can we commit to truly listening to each other when feelings of doubt and insecurity creep up?

10) Can we stay focused on our relationship, which is real and involves a true partnership, or are we in any danger of believing the old saying that the "grass is greener on the other side"?

For some people, sex can really just be sex. However, there's a danger of developing true feelings for the other person. If you're interested in preserving your own relationship, it's vital to construct an emotional barrier from your recreational sex partner. It's sex and only sex. You're not there to listen to him or her complain about his spouse. You're not there to offer a sympathetic ear over a cup of coffee. You're just there for sex. If you find yourself meeting the other person "just to talk" without your wife/husband/girlfriend/boyfriend knowing about it, you're in trouble.

8 TAKING A BREAK

There are many reasons for wanting to take a break from partner swapping. You might have sudden health problems that demand your attention, family responsibilities come into play, or maybe you've just had enough of it and want to reconnect with your own partner on a deeper level. The important thing is being able to articulate your reasons to your partner. Remember the Boundary Contract you and your partner completed earlier? This might be a good time to dig it out, especially if you have specifically designed ways of "opting out".

Discuss the following points with your partner if you've reached the point where you no longer want to engage in partner swapping, whether it's a decision you think might be permanent, or whether you simply want to take a break.

1) I'm ready to take a break from partner swapping and here are my reasons...

2) I'd like the swapping to end immediately, next week, next month, etc.

3) Are you ready to take a break as well, or do you want to try and convince me to continue?

4) Do you promise not to pressure me to continue partner swapping if I'm truly ready for it to end?

5) We've spent a fair bit of energy investing our sexual selves with other people. What can we do now to reinvest that time and intimacy with our own relationship?

6) Do you agree that we should notify the other couple(s) together to let them know that we're not longer interested in swapping?

7) Are we both prepared to walk away from the swapping couples with the understanding that we were only involved in their lives for sexual recreation and nothing more?

8) If the swapping partners have also been our close friends for years, how do we suddenly separate sex from our friendship while still maintaining a friendship with them?

9) Do we anticipate animosity from the other couple and, if so, how are we going to deal with that?

10) Do we want to set a date to revisit the idea of partner swapping again at some point in the future or are we truly done with it?

How you handle taking a break is vital to the strength of your relationship. It takes a lot of trust, honesty, and respect to be able to give up your own pleasure for the sake of your partner's well-being. The whole idea of partner-swapping is that you enter into it with eyes fully opened to the possibilities, and come out of it with your relationship unscathed. Remember, these questions are meant to guide your conversation, not monopolize it. Expand on the topics, discuss anything that's important to you at this time. Listen to your partner and respect what he or she has to say.

Ultimately, the questions in this book aren't all inclusive. They're meant to get you talking, and hopefully they've done just that. Take your time. Talk a lot. Talk some more. Make sure you've really got a handle on what partner swapping means.

PARTNER SWAPPING ARE YOU READY?

ABOUT THE AUTHOR

L.A. Theriault has written articles for regional, provincial, and national magazines. Works of fiction have been published both in print and online.

www.ingramcontent.com/pod-product-compliance
Lightning Source LLC
Chambersburg PA
CBHW070254290526
45789CB00004B/1854